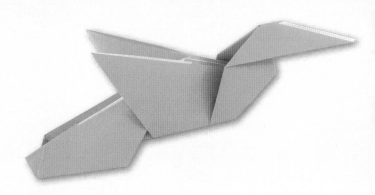

easy Origami
for beginners

Full-color instructions for 20 simple projects

Michael G. LaFosse

TUTTLE Publishing

Tokyo | Rutland, Vermont | Singapore

contents

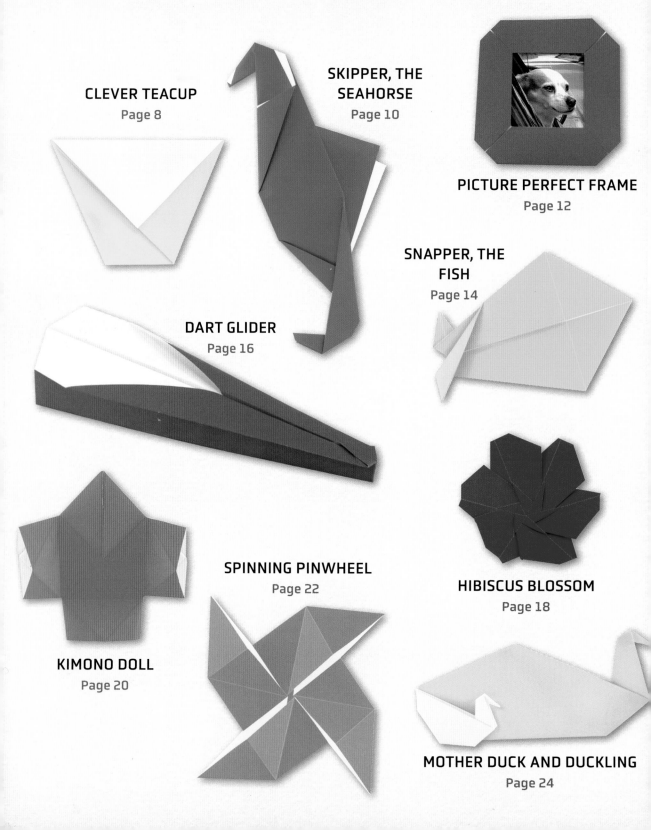

Introduction

The idea of folding paper is as old as paper itself. Think of the advantages to early folders: Folding a message kept its contents secret. Wrapped goods stayed clean and fresh. Written accounts were more convenient to carry and read when folded into a book, instead of being rolled into a scroll.

With the development of origami, paper became much more than a simple wrapper or convenience. The artful folds form models that garner admiration and inspire imitation. Beautiful patterns emerge, and representations of living things and familiar or clever objects take form.

Origami is wonderfully simple. The folder needs nothing more than something to fold—no glue or tape—just paper! Origami exemplifies the mind's ability to solve problems and create harmony. Folding is relaxing, but it is also exciting to invent new ways to fold paper.

The Chinese are credited with the invention of paper, and they were probably the first to create folded paper designs. But today, paper folding is known the world over by its Japanese name. This is thanks to the venerable Japanese origami crane, one of the most popular designs ever made. When modern folders needed a simple word for their art, they looked to Japan, the home of the folded paper crane, and came up with *origami*. In Japanese *ori* means "to fold" and *kami* means "paper."

Origami Paper

Choosing the best paper for a particular project can be as important as the folding process itself. Here are some things to consider:

Paper for learning and practicing origami does not have to be fancy or expensive. Look for papers that are fairly thin, like copier paper or sheets cut from the pages of discarded magazines. You must, of course, prepare your papers: cut them carefully to make perfect squares.

When you're ready to build a collection of fine folding papers, you'll discover many options that you can order online: machine made and handmade, in rolls or sheets, and in many colors, patterns and sizes.

Terazaki / Wikimedia Commons (by way of The Metropolitan Museum of Art, a gift of Lincoln Kirstein, 1959) / Public Domain

How to Fold 1
RECOGNIZING THE SYMBOLS

By making this simple Flower Bud, you will learn how to recognize the origami diagram symbols listed to the right.

- Valley fold
- Mountain fold
- Follow this spot
- Rotate symbol
- Fold and unfold arrow
- Fold in front arrow
- Fold behind arrow

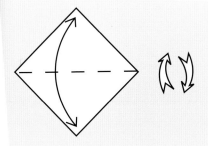

1 Begin with a square piece of paper, white side up if you are using origami paper. Fold the paper in half bottom corner to the top corner, and then unfold. Here you see what the valley fold (dashed line) is and what the fold and unfold arrow looks like. Next, notice the rotate symbol to the right of the diagram. This indicates that you must position your paper to look like step 2 (with the crease running vertically) before making the next fold.

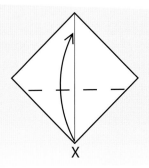

2 By now, you should have rotated your paper so that the crease made in step 1 is running from the top corner to the bottom corner. Now, lift up the bottom corner to make a fold, but do not lift it all the way to the top. See the X, "follow this spot," symbol at the bottom corner. You need to look ahead to step 3 to see where the X should go.

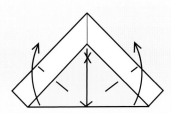

3 Fold up the left and right sides. Here, there is no X on the left and right sides. Even without the X, it is a good habit to look ahead to the next step, so you will be able to see what the paper should look like after following the instructions.

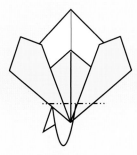

4 Fold the bottom corner to the back. Here, you see the mountain fold indicator (a broken dashed line) and the open half arrow indicating that you should "fold behind."

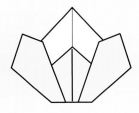

5 Now you have the finished Flower Bud! Make several tiny buds from two-inch square papers and paste them onto the front of a handmade card, or save them to decorate another project.

How to Fold 2
PRACTICING NEAT FOLDING

Neatness is important when you are folding. This simple exercise will help you practice matching edges—a straightforward task but a common problem for many beginners who do not realize how important it will become later on.

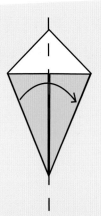

3 Fold the Kite Base in half left to right. This is a good way to check for neatness. Do all of the edges match? Are the corners neat?

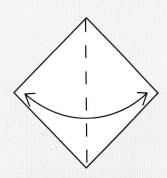

1 Begin with a square of paper, white side up if you are using origami paper. Fold it in half corner to corner, and then unfold. Be sure to match the corners and the edges of the square carefully before you press the paper flat to "commit" the crease.

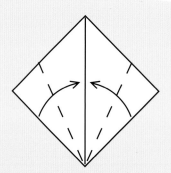

2 Fold the two bottom edges to meet at the crease in the center. For neatness, fold only one side at a time. Leave an approximately one-millimeter gap between the two folded flap edges (to facilitate the fold in step 3), but be sure that the edges of the paper align with the crease exactly before you press the paper flat. This shape is often called the "Kite Base." Many origami designs begin from this basic shape.

4 Make several of these and use them to practice inside reverse folding, as explained in the next section, where you will make an origami Duck!

How did you do? If your shape is not very tidy, try to determine what went wrong. Perhaps your paper is the problem. Check to see if it is really square. If the paper is square, perhaps your first fold, from step 1, was done poorly—every fold counts! Try again. Practice will help you improve your basic folding skills. Teaching others what you have learned will improve these skills, too.

How to Fold 3
LEARNING THE INSIDE REVERSE FOLD

In this section you will practice the inside reverse fold. This is an important origami technique that, with a little practice, will allow you to complete many origami designs. The inside reverse fold is most often used to make bends in the paper for the joints of the limbs, neck and head of an origami animal.

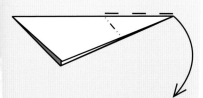

1 Begin with a Kite Base folded in half (see the facing page for the folding method). Here, you see a typical drawing of an inside reverse fold instruction. Look at step 4 to see what the paper should look like once it has been inside reverse folded. Notice that the corner has been bent inside itself.

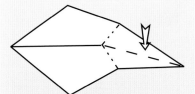

2 Begin the fold by opening the Kite Base from underneath. Now you can easily push the narrow end downward. Notice that only part of the Kite Base will be valley folded, from the bend in the middle to the end of the point.

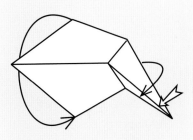

3 Once the valley fold portion of the fold is started, you can begin to fold the shape flat (in half) again. You can push the bent point to any angle you want.

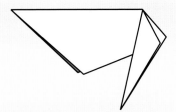

4 This is what a completed inside reverse fold should look like.

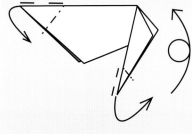

5 Try adding two more inside reverse folds, one at the left end and another at the end you folded in steps 1–3. Notice the "turn the paper over" symbol, which tells you that after you make the inside reverse folds, you should turn the paper over so it looks like the next drawing.

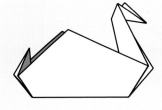

6 This is your finished Duck! Make many of them to become an expert at inside reverse folding.

Clever Teacup

Traditional Design

Michael folded and filled this model from his school's water cooler, amazing his friends. As an origami fan, you will probably have paper, which is handy when you want to share drink from a larger container. Waxed paper from the kitchen makes a longer lasting cup, but be careful not to use fancy papers with water-soluble dyes, coatings or glitter!

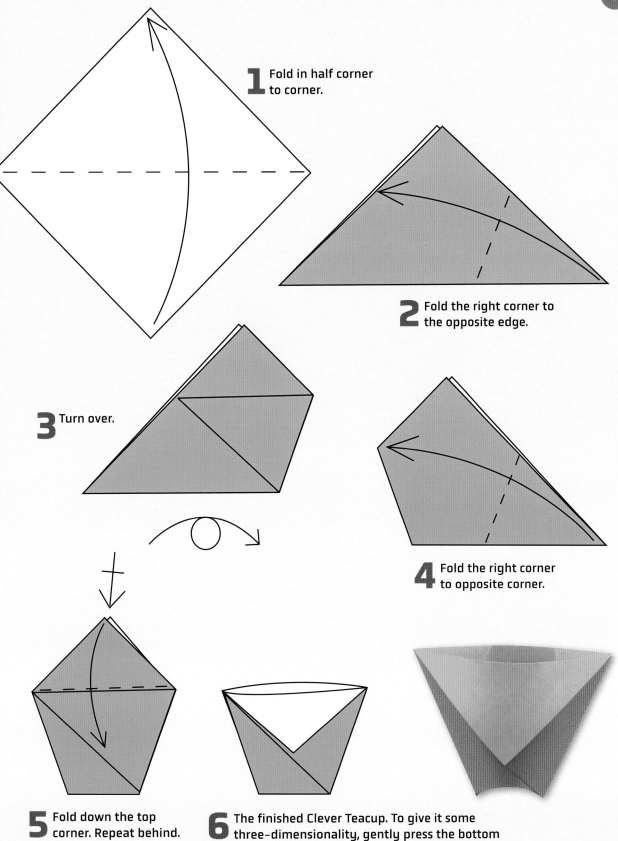

1 Fold in half corner to corner.

2 Fold the right corner to the opposite edge.

3 Turn over.

4 Fold the right corner to opposite corner.

5 Fold down the top corner. Repeat behind.

6 The finished Clever Teacup. To give it some three-dimensionality, gently press the bottom edge inside the container, forming a curved area. Encourage the lip to take on a rounded shape.

Skipper, the Seahorse

Designed by Michael G. LaFosse

Seven simple folds are all that's needed to transform a square of paper
into an expressive seahorse form!

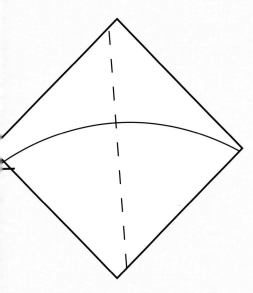

1 Fold in half. Do not match corners.

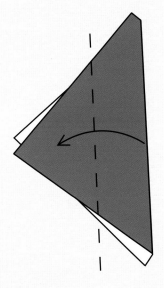

2 Fold over.

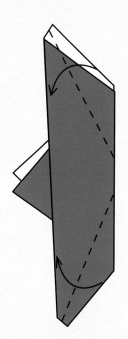

3 Fold the top and bottom edges to the common folded edge.

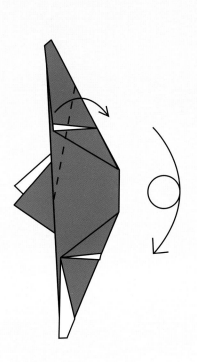

4 Fold the tapered top end over. Turn over top to bottom.

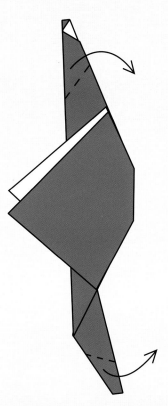

5 Fold down the tapered top end to form the head. Fold up the tapered bottom end for the tail.

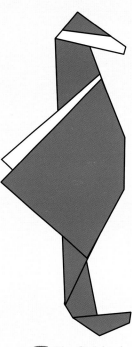

6 The finished Skipper, the Seahorse.

Picture Perfect Frame

Traditional design

It is often said that the frame makes the art, and this origami addition will conceal and protect the raw edges of a favorite photo or drawing. Affix the mount to the frame, and not to the photo or art. This preserves the art from sticky tape or glue. A standard 6-inch (15-cm) square frames a 2¼-inch (5.5-cm) photo. Use that ratio to select larger paper for larger objects. Use decorative papers, or color your own.

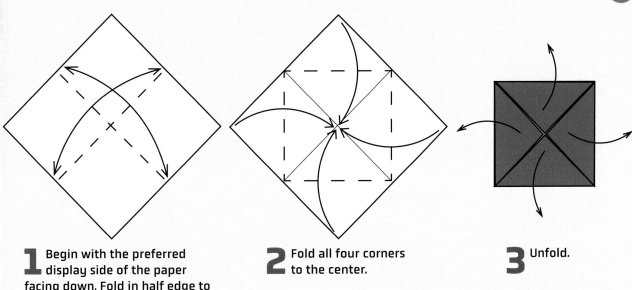

1 Begin with the preferred display side of the paper facing down. Fold in half edge to edge both ways and unfold.

2 Fold all four corners to the center.

3 Unfold.

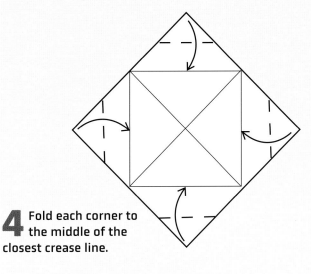

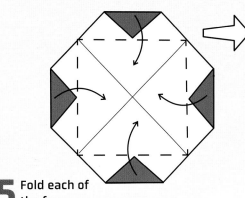

4 Fold each corner to the middle of the closest crease line.

5 Fold each of the four edges over.

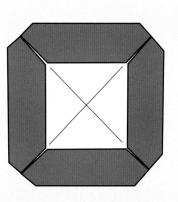

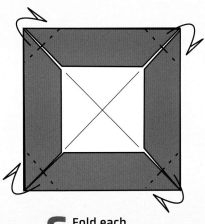

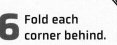

6 Fold each corner behind.

7 The finished Picture Perfect Frame.

Snapper, the Fish

Designed by Michael G. LaFosse

This model employs a clever pivot in step 5 to form its kite-like shape. You can open and close the mouth of this easy action model simply by flexing the tail fins apart and back together.

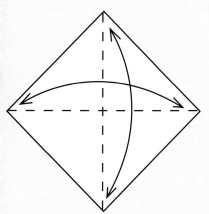

1 With the preferred display side facing down, fold in half corner to corner both ways.

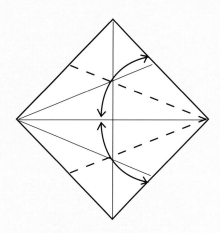

2 Fold two edges from the left side to meet at the crease. Unfold.

3 Fold two edges from the right side to meet at the crease. Unfold.

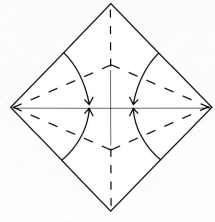

4 Fold all four edges to meet at the horizontal crease. The flaps will rise up where these folds meet.

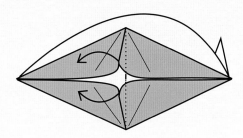

5 Fold in half, with the long edges swinging behind to the right and the short edges pivoting to the left.

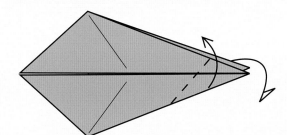

6 Fold the front tail point up and fold the back tail point down.

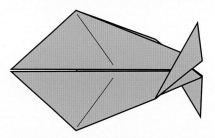

7 The finished Snapper, the Fish. Move the tail fins apart horizontally to make the mouth open and close.

Dart Glider

Traditional Italian design

This classic paper toy is known the world around, and may well be the first origami that many people learn. We have folded the tip inward at step 5 to increase the weight of the nose while blunting an otherwise delicate crumple zone. Tweak the back edges to make the nose pitch up or down, or make the plane bank left or right. Launch several stacked piggy-back, and watch them separate and disperse.

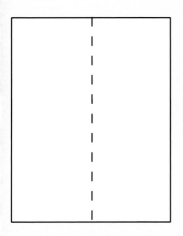

1 Begin with a piece of 8.5"
x 11" computer paper.
Fold in half long edge to long
edge and unfold.

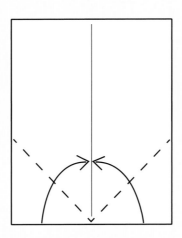

2 Fold up the bottom
corners, making them
meet at the crease.

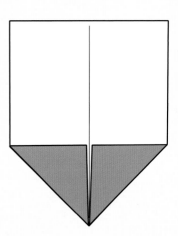

3 Your paper should look
like this.

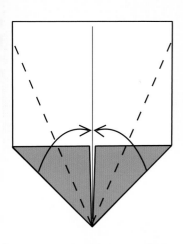

4 Fold in the bottom folded
edges to meet at the crease.

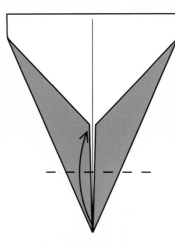

5 Fold up the
bottom corner.

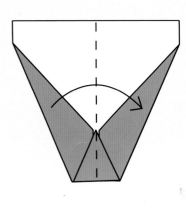

6 Fold in half.

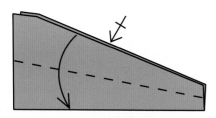

7 Fold down the wings,
one to each side.

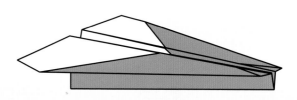

8 The finished Dart Glider.
Open the wings and
throw!

Hibiscus Blossom

Designed by Michael G. LaFosse

This beautiful modular flower requires six sheets of square paper. Each of the petals are folded individually, and then they are cleverly assembled using a series of simple locking folds.

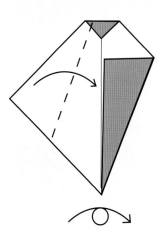

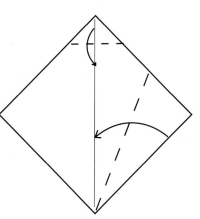

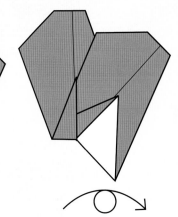

1 Fold and unfold in half corner to corner.

2 Fold the bottom right edge to the center crease. Fold down the top corner. There is no landmark for this approximate fold.

3 Fold the top left edge to the center crease. Turn over left to right.

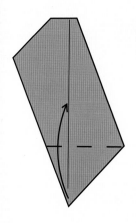

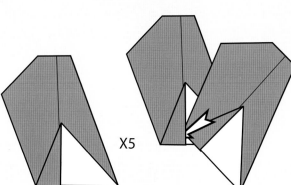

4 Fold up the bottom corner, making the crease run through the right corner while the bottom corner touches the center crease.

5 Make five more of these petal units.

6 Insert the bottom left corner of a unit into the triangle-shaped pocket of another. Notice that the square corners of the triangle pocket must meet. Turn the assembly over.

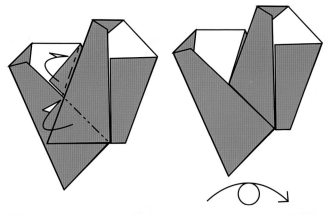

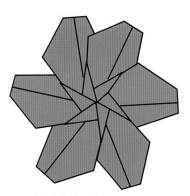

7 Mountain fold the bottom corner over to trap the layer of paper behind it. Mountain fold the other corner in a similar manner. Turn the assembly over and repeat steps 6 and 7 with the remaining pieces. The flower will not lie flat. Let it cup into a 3-D blossom form.

8 The finished Hibiscus Blossom. You may use glue to fortify the connections if you wish.

Kimono Doll

Traditional Japanese design

This charming Japanese paper doll is clothed in the straight-cut, wide-sleeved traditional kimono. The arms can be bent, narrowed or otherwise modified so that different poses of these stylized, human forms can be juxtaposed in interesting ways.

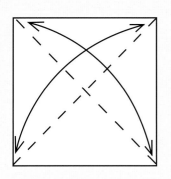

1 Begin with the non-display side facing up. Fold in half corner to corner both ways and unfold.

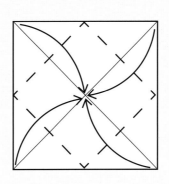

2 Fold all four corners to the center.

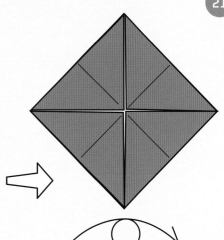

3 Turn over.

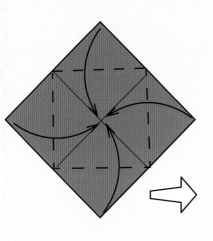

4 Fold all four corners to the center.

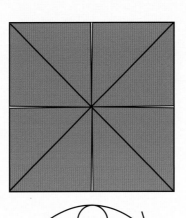

5 Turn over.

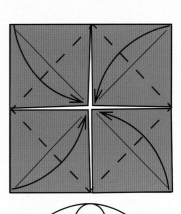

6 Fold all four corners to the center. Turn over.

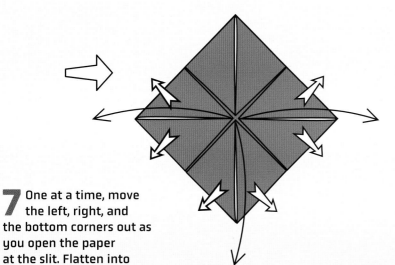

7 One at a time, move the left, right, and the bottom corners out as you open the paper at the slit. Flatten into rectangular shapes.

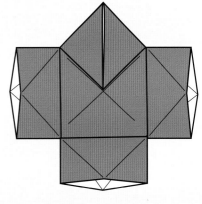

8 The finished Kimono Doll.

Spinning Pinwheel

Traditional design

As a child, I planted colorful origami pinwheels in the yard, enjoying their motion in a gentle breeze. I mounted each pinwheel to a pencil, pushing a pin through the center and into the eraser, and then poking the sharpened pencil tips into the lawn. If you're planning to use your pinwheel outside, keep in mind that folding it from stiffer, plasticized paper will make it last much longer.

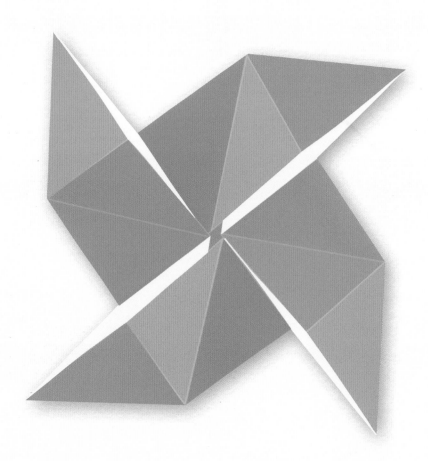

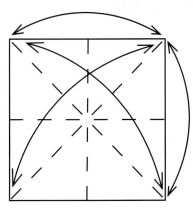

1 Begin with the non-display side facing up. Valley fold in half corner to corner and edge to edge in all four directions.

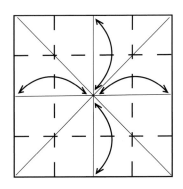

2 Fold and unfold each edge to the center. Turn over.

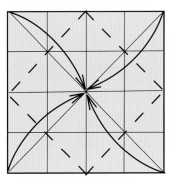

3 Fold all four corners to the center.

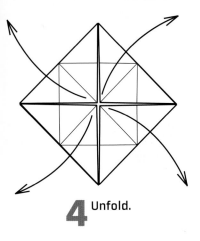

4 Unfold.

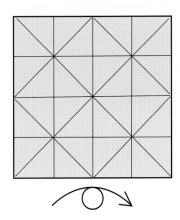

5 Your paper will look like this. Turn over.

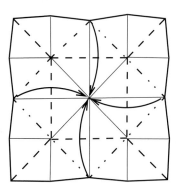

6 Using the crease pattern, bring the center of all four edges to meet at the middle of the paper. Let each corner fold in half.

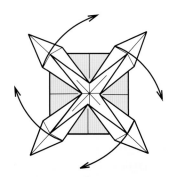

7 Fold each corner over clockwise.

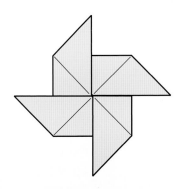

8 The finished Spinning Pinwheel.

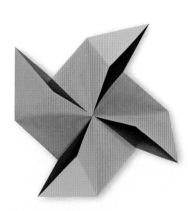

Mother Duck and Duckling

Designed by Michael G. LaFosse

There are plenty of origami bird designs to be had, and even several different origami ducks to choose from, but this charming, simple origami model pairs a mother duck with her duckling using only one sheet of paper!

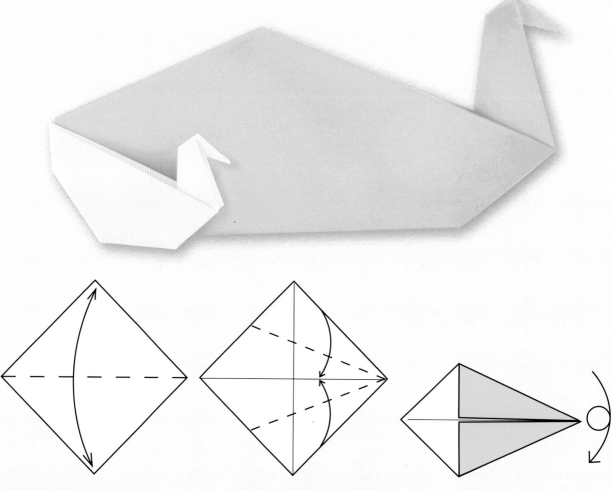

1 With the mother duck color side of the paper facing down, fold in half bottom corner to top corner. Unfold.

2 Valley fold the right edges to the horizontal crease to make a Kite Base.

3 Turn over, top to bottom.

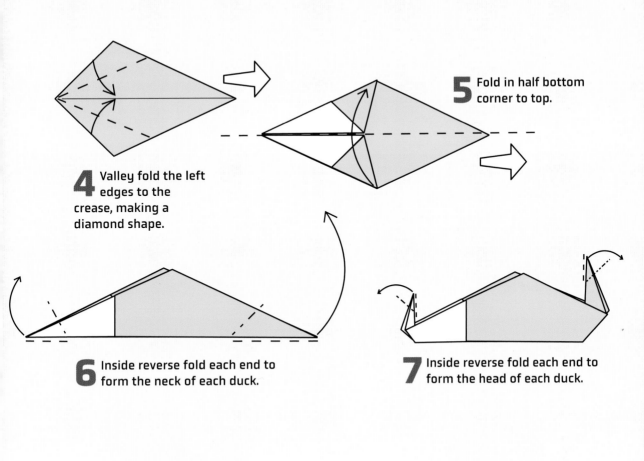

4 Valley fold the left edges to the crease, making a diamond shape.

5 Fold in half bottom corner to top.

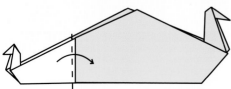

6 Inside reverse fold each end to form the neck of each duck.

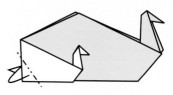

7 Inside reverse fold each end to form the head of each duck.

8 Fold the baby duck over the back end of the mother duck.

9 Mountain fold the back corner behind.

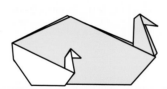

10 The finished Mother Duck and Duckling.

Classic Sailboat

Designed by Michael G. LaFosse

Simple and fun to fold, there's a reason why this model was chosen to be the logo for OrigamiUSA. You can complete this model with symmetrical sails, or customize it with a shorter headsail.

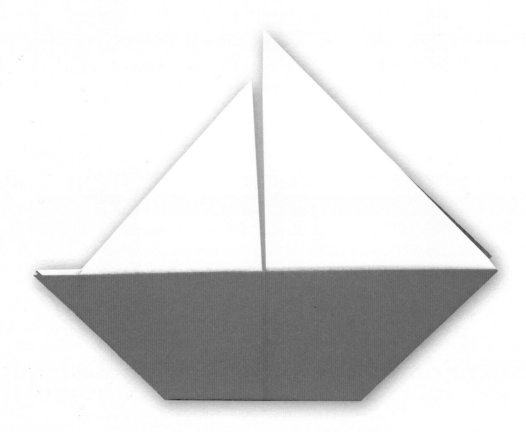

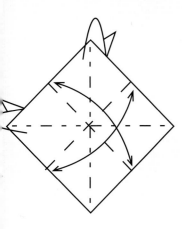

1 With the preferred sail color side facing up, make mountain folds corner to corner, and valley folds edge to edge.

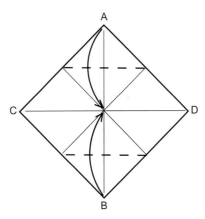

2 Fold the A and B corners to meet at the center of the paper.

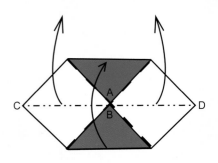

3 Mountain fold from C to D, bringing the points together to make the sails. Use the valley creases along the A and B edges to flatten the boat.

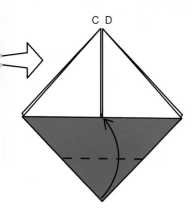

4 Your paper should look like this. Fold up the bottom corner.

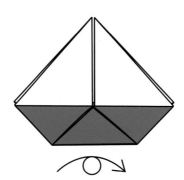

5 Turn over.

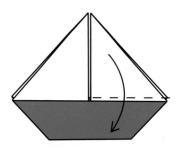

6 Here you have a sailboat. To make one sail smaller than the other, fold the right sail down.

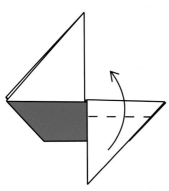

7 Fold some of it back up.

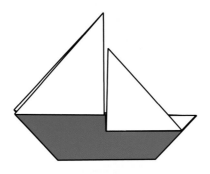

8 Tuck the bottom edge of the folded sail inside the boat.

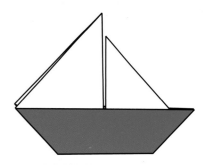

9 The finished Classic Sailboat.

The Japanese Crane

Traditional Japanese design

No other model is as beloved as this traditional Japanese crane. From one point of view, it is a remarkable example of both engineering and art. No one knows who deserves the praise and credit, yet centuries later, this gift continues to delight folders with the magic of origami.

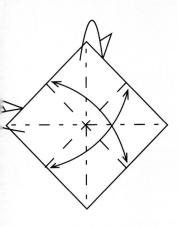 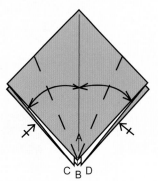 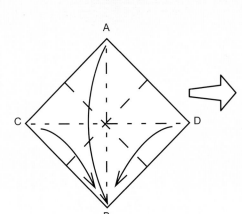

1 With the non-display side facing up, make mountain folds corner to corner, and valley folds edge to edge.

2 Mountain fold the C and D corners, bringing A, C and D down to B.

3 Your paper should look like this. Fold and unfold the bottom open edges to the crease. Repeat behind.

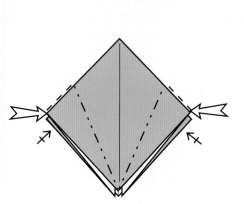 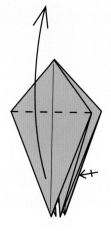 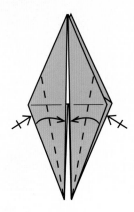

4 Inside reverse fold the corners, following the creases from step 3. Repeat behind.

5 Fold up the front flap. Repeat behind.

6 Fold in the bottom edges, two in the front and two in the back.

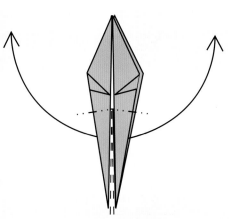 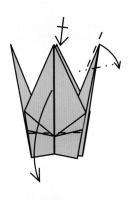 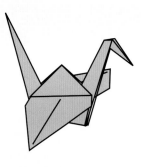

7 Inside reverse fold the bottom corners.

8 Inside reverse fold one corner for the beak. Fold down the wings.

9 The finished Japanese Crane.

Flash, the Firefly

Designed by Michael G. LaFosse

Make sure you have the brighter side of your paper facing up when you begin folding so the firefly's abdomen is "lit" in the finished piece. For a special effect, try using paper stained with fluorescent dye, or even a glow-in-the-dark treatment.

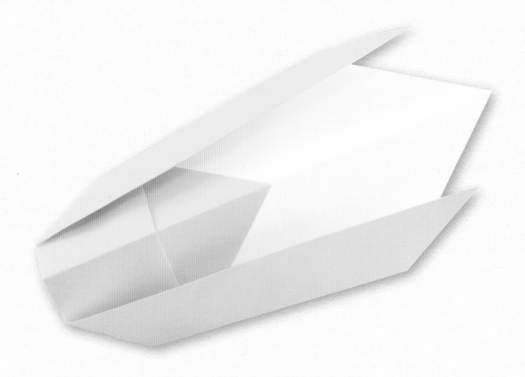

Use a 2-inch (5-cm) sheet for a life-size firefly.

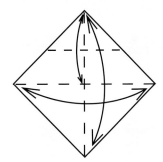

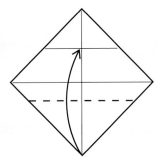

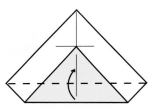

1 Begin white side up, if you are using paper that is printed on only one side. Fold in half diagonally both ways, and then unfold. Fold the top corner to the center, and then unfold.

2 Fold the bottom corner up to the topmost intersection of creases.

3 Fold up the bottom edge using the existing horizontal crease.

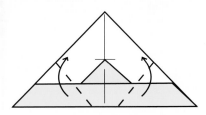

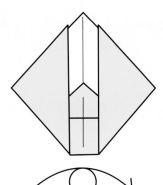

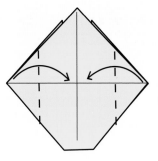

4 Fold up the left and right corners. Align the edges to the top corner but leave a gap, showing the white paper for the abdomen. Look ahead to step 5 for the shape.

5 Turn over left to right.

6 Fold in the left and right corners to meet at the center.

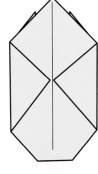

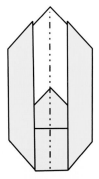

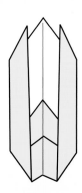

7 Turn over left to right.

8 Mountain fold along the vertical center line.

9 The finished Flash, the Firefly.

Henrietta Hen

Designed by Michael G. LaFosse

With all its varied planes and angles, this is a rather complex-looking model. But don't be intimidated—it's surprisingly easy and enjoyable to fold. Begin with the head–back–tail color facing up.

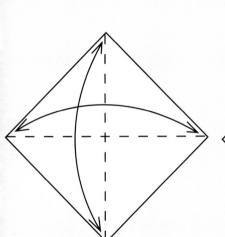

1 Fold in half corner to corner both ways. Unfold.

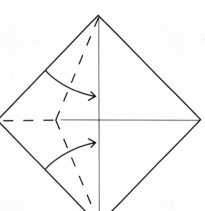

2 Fold the top and bottom left edges to the vertical crease. A flap will lift up in the middle.

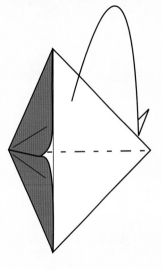

3 Mountain fold in half.

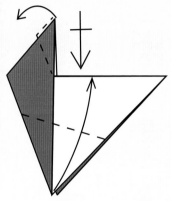

4 Outside reverse fold the top corner to make the beak. Fold up the wings on each side.

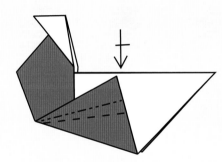

5 Mountain and valley fold the wings to make them pleated.

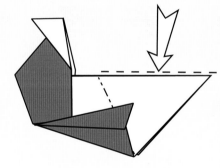

6 Inside reverse fold the tail down.

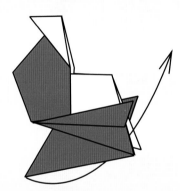

7 Inside reverse fold the tail up.

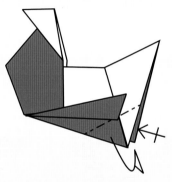

8 Mountain fold the back corners in.

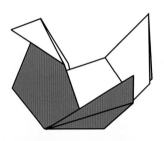

9 The finished Henrietta Hen.

Lotus Flower

Traditional design

Opening out the layers from this classic base produces a series of petals resembling a blooming lotus flower. You might glue two back to back with a ribbon loop between to serve as a holiday ornament. Insert a small square of contrasting color foil (or even a small photo) into the white center before refolding the lotus to add flair or a personal element of interest.

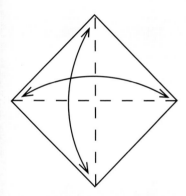

1 Begin with the non-primary display side facing up. Fold in half corner to corner both ways and unfold.

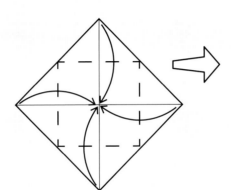

2 Fold all four corners to the center.

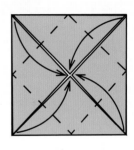

3 Fold all four corners to the center.

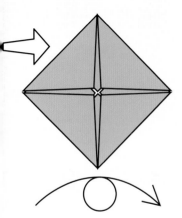

4 Turn over.

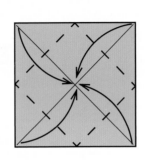

5 Fold all four corners to the center.

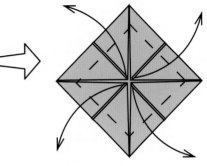

6 Fold out each corner partway to form an 8-pointed star.

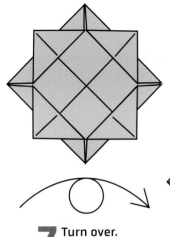

7 Turn over.

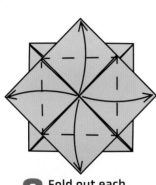

8 Fold out each corner.

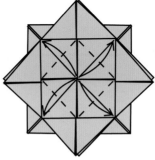

9 Fold out each corner.

10 The finished Lotus Flower.

Jumping Frog

Designed by Michael G. LaFosse

This action-model becomes a fun game of skill. Cut a square from a magazine's reader reply card (or other stiff paper). After a few easy folds, stretch the pleated spring slightly. Apply pressure while you stroke your index finger down the frog's back. When your finger slides off the end, it will cause the frog to spring forward. See how far away you can launch your frog or try to hop it into a target dish "pond."

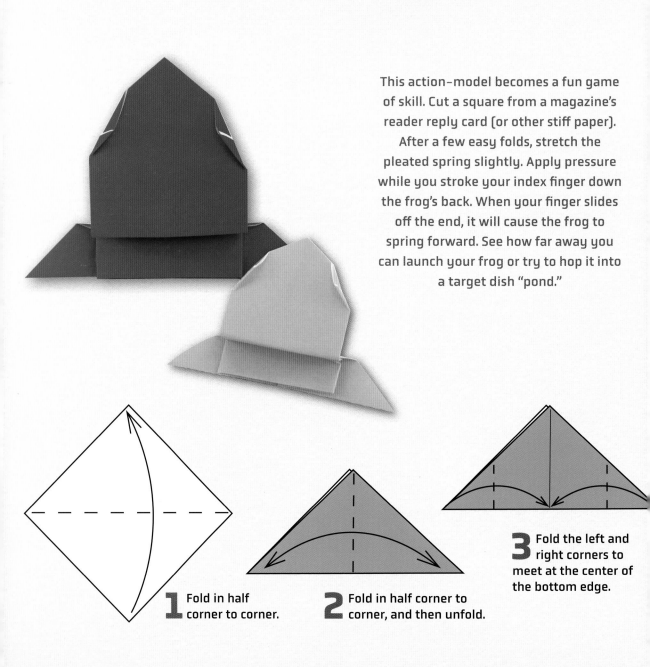

1 Fold in half corner to corner.

2 Fold in half corner to corner, and then unfold.

3 Fold the left and right corners to meet at the center of the bottom edge.

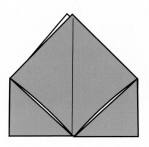

4 Turn over.

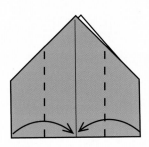

5 Fold the edges to meet in the middle. Let the corners come out from behind.

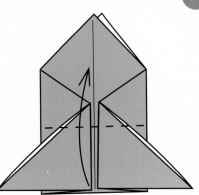

6 Your paper will look like this. Fold up the bottom edge.

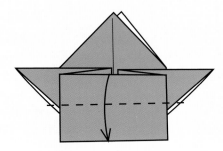

7 Fold down to the bottom edge.

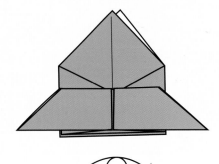

8 Turn over.

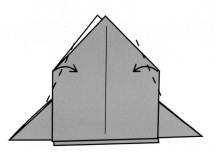

9 Fold over paper for the eyes.

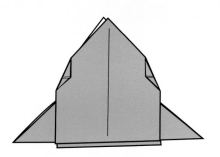

10 The finished Jumping Frog. Press down and slide your finger off the edge of the back end to make it jump!

Snazzy Star Box

Traditional design

This festive container is one of the many origami models that begin in the same way as the traditional Japanese Crane. Because of the Crane's popularity, the Star Box is perhaps the most popular origami box. Festive two-colored papers make great party favors, whether filled with tasty treats or fragrant potpourri. See if you can fold the flaps together to close the container in an interesting way.

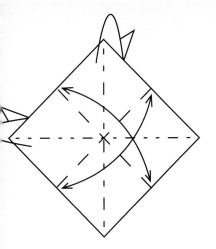

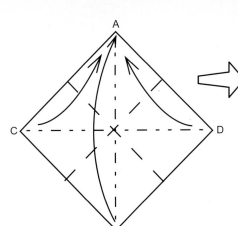

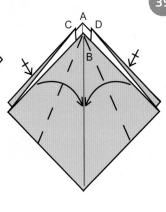

1 With the box interior color side facing up, make mountain folds corner to corner both ways, and valley folds edge to edge both ways.

2 Mountain fold the C and D corners, bringing B, C and D up to A.

3 Your paper should look like this. Fold the top edges to meet at the vertical crease. Repeat behind.

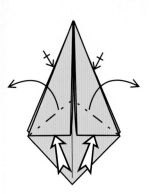

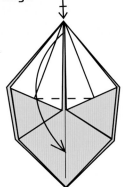

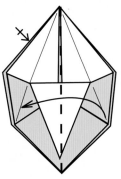

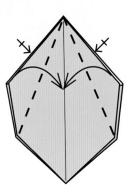

4 One at a time, push open the triangular flaps, separating the layers and flattening them to resemble the shapes in step 5. Repeat behind.

5 Fold down the top corner. Repeat behind.

6 Fold the top layer of the right side over to the left. Repeat behind.

7 Fold in the top edges to meet at the crease. Repeat behind.

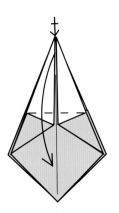

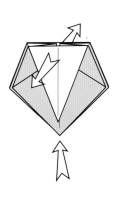

8 Fold down the top corner. Repeat behind.

9 Pull open the sides as you push the bottom flat.

10 The finished Snazzy Star Box.

Pagoda Tower

Traditional Chinese design

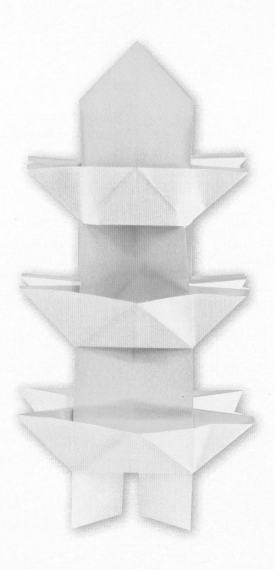

This modular origami model requires that you stack at least a few units to create a replica of an Asian tower or temple. Try experimenting with using smaller and smaller papers as you fold ascending levels.

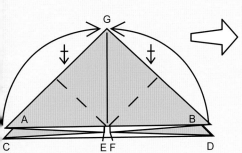

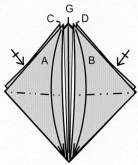

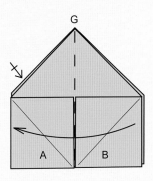

1 Begin by completing the first two steps of the Inflatable Balloon Bunny (page 47). Fold A and B up to G. Repeat behind with C and D.

2 One at a time, bring corners A and B to the bottom, opening the layers to flatten each into a square shape. Repeat behind.

3 Fold the top layer of the right side over to the left. Repeat behind.

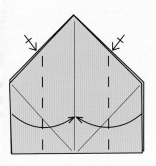

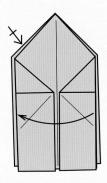

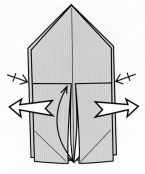

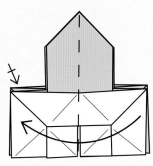

4 Fold the left and the right sides in to meet at the vertical crease. Repeat behind.

5 Fold the top layer of the right side over to the left. Repeat behind.

6 Open the left and right layers out and flatten. Repeat behind.

7 Fold the top layer of the right side over to the left. Repeat behind.

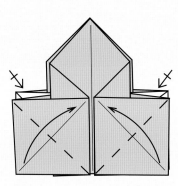

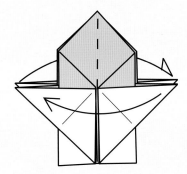

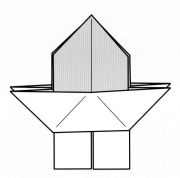

8 Fold up the bottom corners. Repeat behind.

9 Fold the top layer of the right side over to the left. Repeat behind.

10 The finished Pagoda Tower unit. Make several and stack them to form a tower.

Beautiful Butterfly

Designed by Michael G. LaFosse

Also known as "Emiko's Fritillary," this model was originally named for Mrs. Emiko Kruckner, student and American liaison of origami master Akira Yoshizawa.

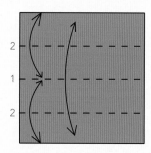

1 Step 1: fold in half edge to edge, and then unfold. Step 2: fold the top and bottom edges to the center. Unfold.

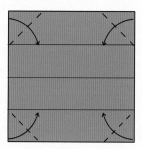

2 Fold all four corners in, stopping at the creases.

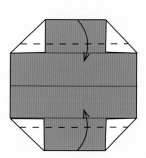

3 Fold the top and bottom edges inward and a little beyond the nearest creases.

The degree to which the flap extends beyond the crease in step 3 will determine the look of the wings. Less overlap will result in pointed wings. More overlap will result in blunted wings. Experiment!

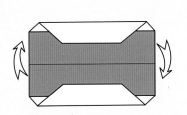

4 Rotate the paper to the vertical orientation.

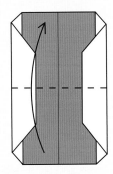

5 Fold in half bottom to top.

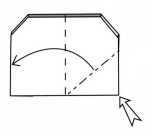

6 Squash fold the right half.

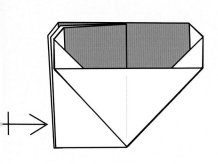

7 Repeat on the other side.

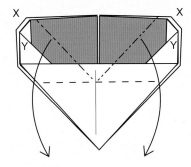

8 Squash fold the left and right wing sections. Watch the X and Y portions—X stays above; Y moves below.

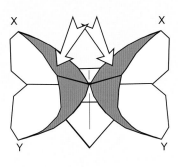

9 Squashing in progress.

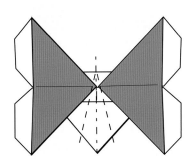

10 Mountain and valley fold the center paper to form the body.

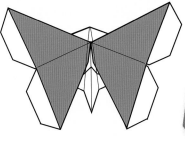

11 The finished Beautiful Butterfly.

Billy, the Toucan

Designed by Michael G. LaFosse

Named "Billy" for his impressive bill, this model calls for rabbit ear folds to create the wings in step 5, followed by a series of reverse folds to shape the body, with an optional sink to blunt the top of the head in step 10. Sinks are challenging, but made easier if you partially unfold the model before you begin the maneuver.

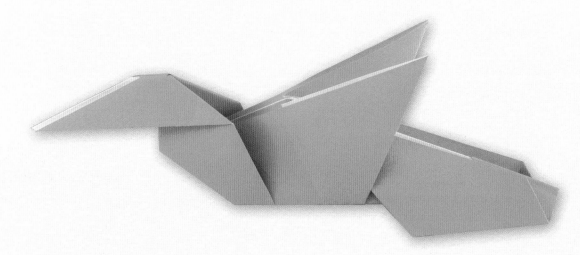

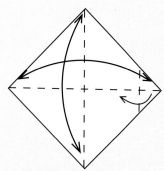

1 Fold in half corner to corner both ways, and then unfold. Fold in the right side corner, about one quarter from the center.

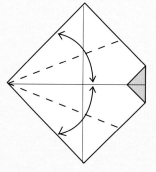

2 Fold in the left side top and bottom edges to meet at the center crease. Unfold.

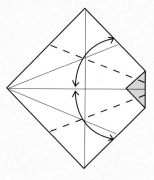

3 Fold in the right side top and bottom edges to meet at the center crease. Unfold.

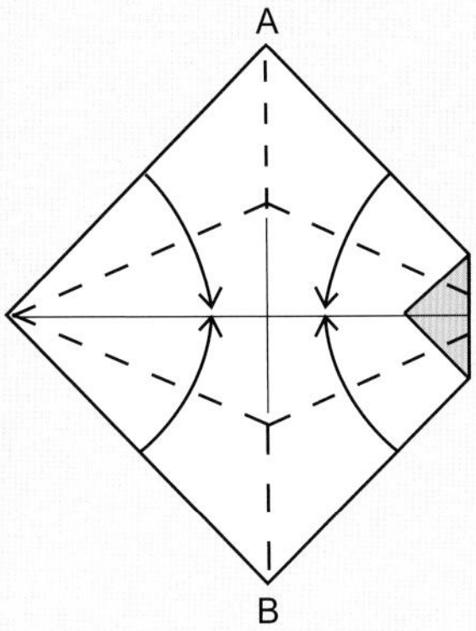

4 Fold all four edges into the center crease, while folding points A and B in half.

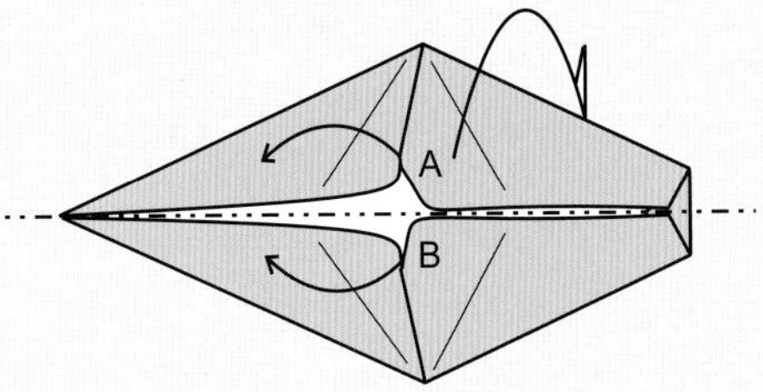

5 Fold A and B to the left. Mountain fold in half.

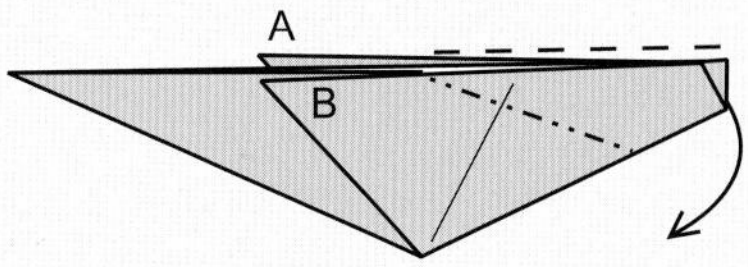

6 Inside reverse fold the right end to form the tail.

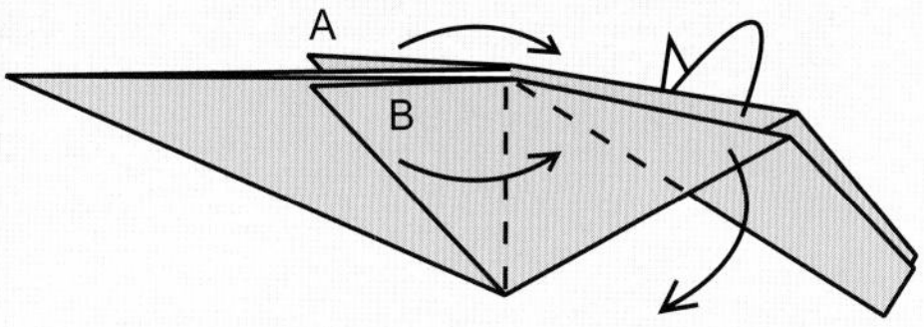

7 Fold over the tail edges, one on each side. Fold A and B to the right.

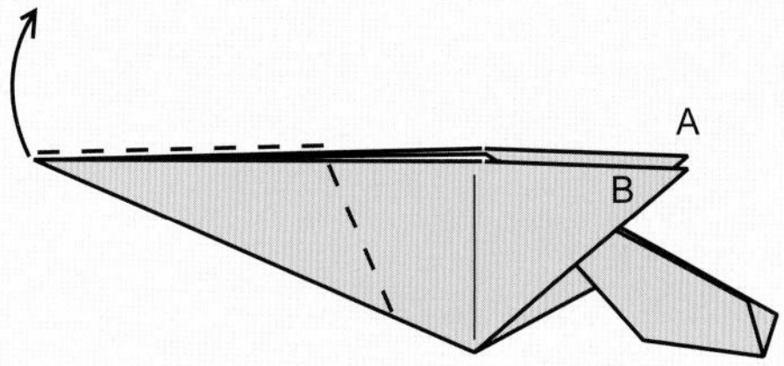

8 Outside reverse fold the left corner to form the neck.

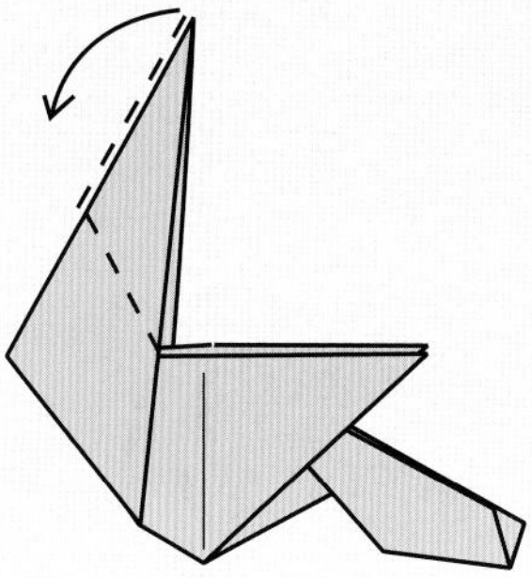

9 Outside reverse fold the neck to form the beak.

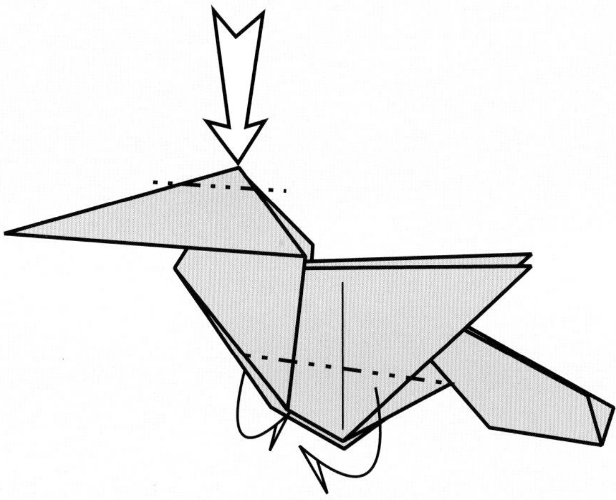

10 Push in the top of the head (optional). Mountain fold the bottom edges inside (optional).

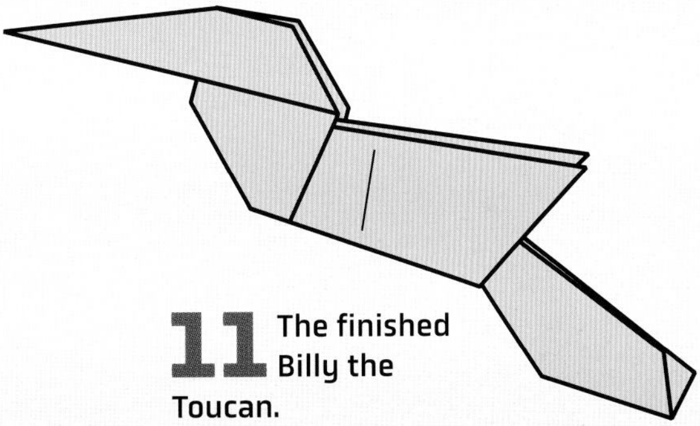

11 The finished Billy the Toucan.

Inflatable Bunny Balloon

Traditional design

One of many delightful variations of the origami balloon, this model utilizes two of the triangular locking flaps to fashion the bunny's ears. This form can either represent an entire baby bunny (with the hole as its mouth), or just a rabbit's head (with the hole behind the neck). To avoid confusion, some folders add eye decorations or a cotton tail to depict which view they prefer.

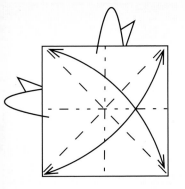 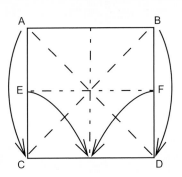 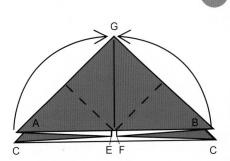

1 With the non-display side facing up, make mountain folds edge to edge, and valley folds corner to corner.

2 Mountain fold the E and F edges, bringing A down to C and B down to D.

3 Fold A and B up to G.

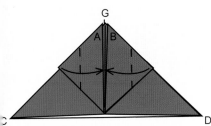 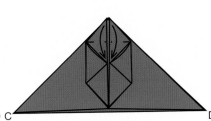 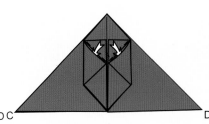

4 Fold in the left and right corners of the upper flaps to meet at the center of the paper.

5 Fold down A and B.

6 Tuck the flaps into the pockets. Turn over.

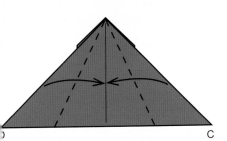 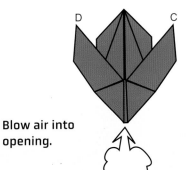 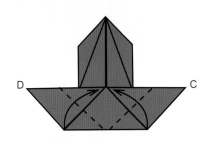

7 Fold edges to meet at the vertical crease.

8 Fold points D and C out to the left and to the right, as far as possible.

9 Fold the bottom corners to meet at the center of the paper.

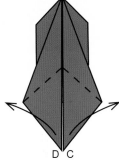

10 Blow air into opening.

11 The finished Inflatable Bunny Balloon.

Michael G. LaFosse has been an origami artist for decades, and is an acknowledged authority and master of the art. An avid teacher, LaFosse co-founded the Origamido Studio, a learning center and design studio dedicated to the art of origami, and the only place in the world specializing in handmade papermaking for the origami artist community. Origamido also produces folded art and commercial designs for a variety of international clients. LaFosse co-curated *Origami Now!*, a wildly popular year-long exhibition at the Peabody Essex Museum in Salem, MA. Vanessa Gould prominently features LaFosse in the Peabody Award-winning film, *Between the Folds*.

The Tuttle Story
"Books to Span the East and West"

Our core mission at Tuttle Publishing is to create books which bring people together one page at a time. Tuttle was founded in 1832 in the small New England town of Rutland, Vermont (USA). Our fundamental values remain as strong today as they were then—to publish best-in-class books informing the English-speaking world about the countries and peoples of Asia. The world has become a smaller place today and Asia's economic, cultural and political influence has expanded, yet the need for meaningful dialogue and information about this diverse region has never been greater. Since 1948, Tuttle has been a leader in publishing books on the cultures, arts, cuisines, languages and literatures of Asia. Our authors and photographers have won numerous awards and Tuttle has published thousands of books on subjects ranging from martial arts to paper crafts. We welcome you to explore the wealth of information available on Asia at **www.tuttlepublishing.com.**

Published in 2020 by Tuttle Publishing, an imprint of Periplus Editions (HK) Ltd.

www.tuttlepublishing.com

Copyright © 2020 Charles E. Tuttle Co.

ISBN 978-0-8048-5193-0

Distributed by

North America, Latin America & Europe
Tuttle Publishing
364 Innovation Drive
North Clarendon, VT 05759-9436 U.S.A.
Tel: (802) 773-8930 | Fax: (802) 773-6993
info@tuttlepublishing.com | www.tuttlepublishing.com

Japan
Tuttle Publishing
Yaekari Building, 3rd Floor
5-4-12 Osaki
Shinagawa-ku
Tokyo 141 0032
Tel: (81) 3 5437-0171 | Fax: (81) 3 5437-0755
sales@tuttle.co.jp | www.tuttle.co.jp

Asia Pacific
Berkeley Books Pte. Ltd.
3 Kallang Sector, #04-01
Singapore 349278
Tel: (65) 6741-2178 | Fax: (65) 6741-2179
inquiries@periplus.com.sg | www.tuttlepublishing.com

Printed in Hong Kong   2006EP
24 23 22 21 20   5 4 3 2 1